EXPLORES ...
ANCIENT GREECE

REMAINS TO BE SEEN
EXPLORING
ANCIENT GREECE

JOHN MALAM

EVANS BROTHERS LIMITED

Acknowledgements

The author and publishers would like to thank the following
people for their valuable help and advice:

Dr K.A. Wardle PhD, Department of Ancient History and
Archaeology, The University of Birmingham.

Illustrations: Jeffery Burn, pages 15 and 21
                    Virginia Gray pages 11,24,33,36-7,38-9
Maps: Jillie Luff, Bitmap Graphics

Editor: Jean Coppendale
Design: Neil Sayer
Production: Peter Thompson

For permission to reproduce copyright material the author and
publishers gratefully acknowledge the following:

Title page: Delphi, the round temple. Travel Photo International

page 8 Ancient Art & Architecture Collection **page 9** (left)
Ancient Art & Architecture Collection, (right) K. Kerth, Zefa
page 10 (top) Ancient Art & Architecture Collection, (bottom)
Travel Photo International **page 11** (top) Ronald Sheridan,
Ancient Art & Architecture Collection, (bottom) Michael Holford
page 12 (top) Michael Holford (bottom) Travel Photo
International **page 13** (bottom left) Peter Clayton, (top left) Mary
Evans Picture Library, (top right) Gordon Urquhart, (bottom
right), Ekdotike Athenon S.A. **page 14** Michael Holford **page 16**
(top left) Michael Holford, (bottom right) Zefa **page 18** (top)
Ronald Sheridan, Ancient Art & Architecture Collection,
(bottom) I.L. Gray-Jones, Trip **page 19** (left) Robert Harding
Picture Library, (right) Michael Holford **page 20** (top) Michael
Holford, (bottom) Ronald Sheridan, Ancient Art & Architecture
Collection **page 21** K. Kerth, Zefa **page 22** (top) Peter Clayton
page 23 (top) E.T. archive, (middle) The Manchester Museum,
(bottom) National Tourist Organisation of Greece **pages 24** (top)
Michelle Jones, Ancent Art & Architecture Collection, (bottom)
Michael Holford **page 26** Ronald Sheridan, Ancient Art &
Architecture Collection **page 27** (top) Michael Holford, (left)
Ronald Sheridan, Ancient Art & Architecture Collection, (bottom
right) E.T. archive **page 28** (top) Helene Rogers, Trip, (bottom
right) Michael Holford **page 29** (bottom left) Ronald Sheridan,
(right) Michael Holford **page 30** Michael Holford **page 31** (top)
Ronald Sheridan, Ancient Art & Architecture Collection, (middle)
Michael Holford, (bottom) Ronald Sheridan, Ancient Art &
Architecture Collection **page 32** (left) Travel Photo International,
(right) Gordon Urquhart **page 33** Michael Holford **page 34** (top
left) Gordon Urquhart, (bottom left and right) Michael Holford
page 35 (left) Peter Clayton, (middle and right) Gordon Urquhart
page 36 Ronald Sheridan, Ancient Art & Architecture Collection
page 38 Michael Holford **page 40** (left) Michael Holford,
(middle) I.L. Gray-Jones, Trip, (right) Peter Clayton **page 41**
(left) Ronald Sheridan, Ancient Art & Architecture Collection
(right) Michael Holford **page 42** (top) Ron Gregory, Lifefile,
(bottom) Helene Rogers, Trip **page 43** (top and bottom) Helene
Rogers, Trip **page 44** Trip **page 45** (top) G. Tortoli, Ancient Art
& Architecture Collection, (bottom left) Peter Terry, Bruce
Coleman Limited, (bottom right) Zefa

Contents

Timeline of Ancient Greece   6

Who were the Greeks?
Introduction to Ancient Greece   8
Map of Greece   9
The Minoan civilization   10
The Mycenaean civilization   12

The world of the Greeks
Dark Age Greece: the time of Homer   14
Archaic Greece: overseas colonies   16
Athens, Sparta and city-states   18
Classical Greece: the 'Golden Age'   20
Macedonian Greece: Philip and Alexander   22

Achievements of the Greeks
Writing and the alphabet   24
Science, medicine and learning   26
Theatre and music   28
Army, navy and fighting   30
Temples and columns   32
Statues and pottery   34

Religion and festivals
Gods and goddesses   36
Myths and legends   38
The Olympic Games   40

The end of Ancient Greece
Greece under the Romans   42
Discovering Ancient Greece   44

Glossary   46

Further reading   47

Index   47

TIMELINE OF ANCIENT GREECE
and the rest of the world

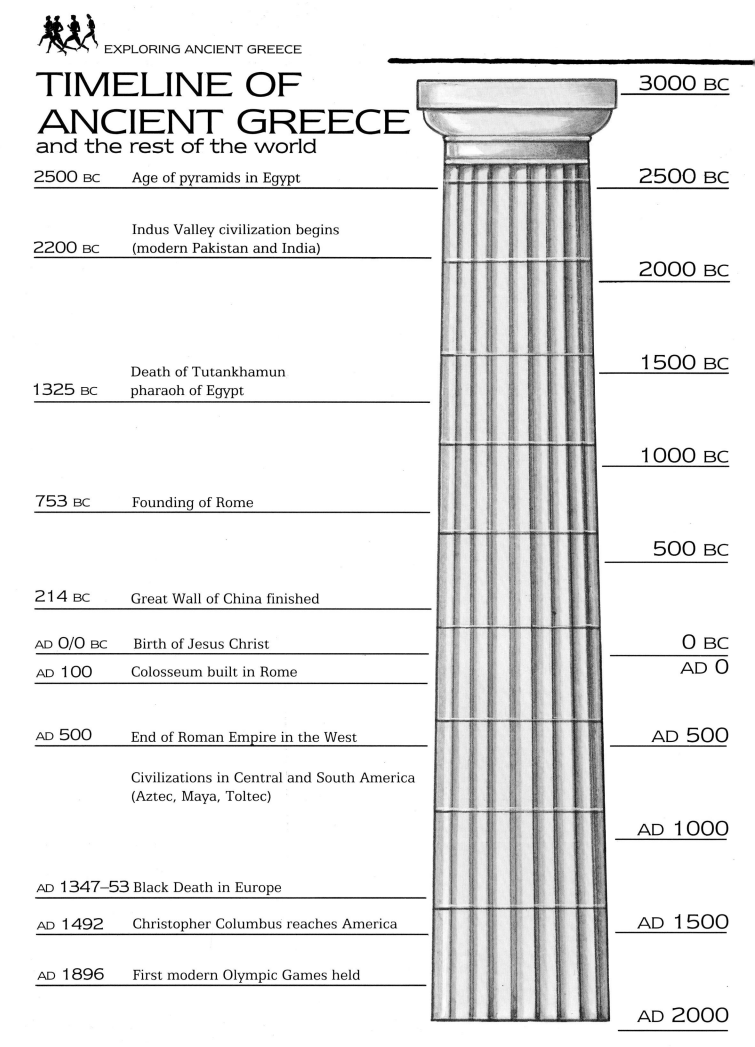

2500 BC — Age of pyramids in Egypt

2200 BC — Indus Valley civilization begins (modern Pakistan and India)

1325 BC — Death of Tutankhamun pharaoh of Egypt

753 BC — Founding of Rome

214 BC — Great Wall of China finished

AD 0/0 BC — Birth of Jesus Christ

AD 100 — Colosseum built in Rome

AD 500 — End of Roman Empire in the West

Civilizations in Central and South America (Aztec, Maya, Toltec)

AD 1347–53 Black Death in Europe

AD 1492 — Christopher Columbus reaches America

AD 1896 — First modern Olympic Games held

3000 BC

2500 BC

2000 BC

1500 BC

1000 BC

500 BC

0 BC

AD 0

AD 500

AD 1000

AD 1500

AD 2000

EARLY BRONZE AGE	Marble figures made by people on the Cyclades Islands.	2900 BC
LATE BRONZE AGE	Emergence of larger communities whose societies were based around palaces. Writing first used during this period. The Minoan civilization flourished on the island of Crete.	
	Volcano destroys Bronze Age towns on the island of Thera. The Mycenaean civilization developed on the mainland.	1600 BC
	Minoan and Mycenaean civilizations ended within a short time of each other.	1100 BC
DARK AGES	A time of hardship and unrest. Bronze Age palaces were abandoned. Writing was forgotten. Poets, such as Homer, told great stories about the past. First Olympic Games held.	700 BC
ARCHAIC PERIOD	A time of recovery. Writing was rediscovered. Colonies were established and prosperity returned.	500 BC
CLASSICAL PERIOD	The 'Golden Age' of Athens and Sparta. After this Alexander the Great won a huge empire.	323 BC
HELLENISTIC PERIOD	The time from Alexander the Great's death until his empire was completely taken over by the Romans.	30 BC
ROMAN PERIOD		

AD 385   Romans abolish the Oracle at Delphi
AD 393   Romans stop the Olympic Games
AD 426   Romans destroy the temples at Olympia
AD 529   Romans close the 'school for thinking' at Athens

Dates

Ancient Greek history is usually divided into several periods, from the Stone Age to the Roman Period. Another way of writing dates is to refer to events before and after the birth of Jesus Christ. Anything before is said to be 'BC' (Before Christ), and anything after is 'AD' (Anno Domini, which is Latin meaning 'in the year of Our Lord').

WHO WERE THE GREEKS?

Introduction to Ancient Greece

Fact File

Islands, seas and mountains

Greece is made up of many islands and a large mainland which is joined to the rest of Europe. There are about 170 inhabited islands and a further 2,000 tiny, uninhabited ones dotted about in the Aegean, Ionian and Mediterranean seas. The mainland and islands often have bare, rocky mountains in the middle and a flatter, fertile plain on the coast. The Greeks have always lived near the sea, and the Ancient Greeks were good sailors. In fact, nowhere in Greece are you more than 100 kilometres from the sea. On the mainland, 80 per cent of the countryside is mountainous, and there are 28 mountains over 2,000 metres high.

Opposite page:
Top left Visitors to the Parthenon in Athens.
Top right An aerial view of one of the Cyclades Islands in the Aegean Sea.

This stone figure was made about 4,500 years ago by people who lived on the Cyclades Islands. It is one of the oldest human figures found in Greece. Its stylized features give it a very 'modern' look. The figure may be a musician, playing a harp.

The first people to live in Greece were hunter-gatherers of the Stone Age. They arrived there about 40,000 years ago, wandering across the land, hunting animals and gathering plants.

About 8,000 years ago, the nomadic lifestyle of the hunter-gatherers began to change. People learned how to grow wheat and barley, and raise sheep and goats. There was no longer any need to roam the land in search of food. From this time onwards the first farming villages were built in Greece.

Some groups of people flourished, such as those who lived on the Cyclades, a group of islands in the Aegean Sea. By 4,500 years ago they were trading with their neighbours on the island of Crete. They exchanged obsidian (a volcanic black glass used to make cutting tools) for pottery and other goods, and they created their own distinctive style of art, as you can see in the picture below.

All these events took place in the prehistoric period – that great stretch of time before humankind learned how to write. It is only after the prehistoric era ended, about 4,000 years ago, that the story of Ancient Greece can really be told, starting with the Minoans who made Crete the centre of their world.

Greece

BULGARIA

ALBANIA

MACEDONIA

• Vergina

▲ Mt Olympus

N

G R E E C E

Ionian Islands

T U R K E Y

• Troy

ASIA
MINOR

AEGEAN
SEA

Chios

• Ephesus

Ikaria

Delphi •   Thebes •
Battle of Chaeronea ✕   ✕ Battle of Marathon 490 BC
338 BC
                    • Athens
Corinth •   ✕ Piraeus
Mycenae •   Battle of Salamis
Tiryns • •   480 BC
Olympia •   Epidavros

Peloponnese

Cyclades Islands

Dodecanese Islands

Naxos

Kos

Taygetos
Mountains   • Sparta

Thera

Rhodes

IONIAN
SEA

Knossos
Gortyn • •
Phaistos •   Crete

MEDITERRANEAN SEA

0   km   200

Map of Greece showing its
mainland part, groups of
islands and places mentioned
in this book.

9

The Minoan civilization

Crete is a good starting point for describing Ancient Greece. It was here that a very early civilization flourished and by learning about it we can begin to answer the question, 'Who were the Greeks?'

In 1900, English archaeologist Sir Arthur Evans discovered the ruins of a royal palace at Knossos, on the north coast of Crete. He linked the palace to the legendary King Minos, from whose name he coined the term 'Minoan'. We don't know what these people called themselves.

The Minoans were a Bronze Age society – in other words they had no knowledge of iron, a much harder metal. Their civilization lasted for 750 years between 2200 and 1450 BC (4,200 to 3,450 years ago). They were farmers who grew wheat, barley, grapes and olives and kept sheep, pigs, goats and cattle.

The Minoans built several palaces and the finest of these was at Knossos. Its walls were decorated with paintings and the streets in the town were paved with stone – perhaps the oldest pavements anywhere in the world. About 30,000 people might have lived at Knossos when it was at its greatest.

About 1450 BC their civilization came to a violent and sudden end. Minoan palaces and towns, including the capital at Knossos, were destroyed by fires. Experts are not sure what caused the fires. Some believe an earthquake started them. Others think Crete was overrun by invaders from mainland Greece called the

The Minoans were expert goldsmiths. This gold pendant shows two bees storing honey in a honeycomb. It is about 3,700 years old.

The Minoan palace of Knossos, built 3,900 years ago. Sir Arthur Evans rebuilt parts of the palace using concrete columns which he painted red and black, the same colours as the original wooden columns. His work helps us to imagine how the palace may have really looked.

Fact File

Early writing

The art of writing reached Greece during the Bronze Age, and was first used on Crete. A system of hieroglyphics was used, possibly adapted from Egyptian symbols. Pictures and symbols were used for words and ideas. The Minoans simplified the hieroglyphics into a script which we call 'Linear A'. In time, this was changed into another script, 'Linear B', by people from the Mycenaean civilization who settled on Crete (see page 12). Two Englishmen, Michael Ventris and John Chadwick, deciphered 'Linear B' in 1952. It is an early type of Greek. The inscriptions are mostly lists of produce such as olives, cereals and sheep, plus references to military equipment such as armour and chariots.

Mycenaeans. About 100 years before the Minoan civilization ended on Crete, a volcano erupted on the nearby island of Thera (nowadays called Santorini). The explosion was so violent that the centre of the island was blown away and towns and villages were lost beneath lava and ash. Excavations on Thera have uncovered a buried town built in the same style as Minoan towns on Crete.

A 'Linear B' tablet recording chariots and horses. The sign in the centre represents a suit of armour similar to the one shown on page 13. 'Linear B' had about 89 different signs in total.

The Phaistos Disk, found at the palace ▶ of Phaistos, the second largest Minoan palace on Crete. It has a hieroglyphic inscription stamped on it using 45 different signs. Both sides are inscribed. It has not been deciphered, though some experts think it is a hymn used in religious services. It was made about 3,600 years ago.

The royal throne found at Knossos – the oldest known throne in Europe. Today, a replica of this throne is used by the President of the International Court at the Hague, Brussels.

The Mycenaean civilization

A clay pot made by the Mycenaeans about 1350 BC. It shows men in chariots. Compare the chariots and horses to the ones on the 'Linear B' tablet on page 11.

The early kings of Mycenae were buried at the bottom of deep shafts within this grave circle. A second grave circle lay outside the walls of the city.

At the same time as the Minoans existed on Crete, a separate civilization emerged on the Greek mainland. This was the Mycenaean civilization, which prospered in the Greek Bronze Age, from about 1600 BC (3,600 years ago).

Like the Minoans, the Mycenaeans built cities and royal palaces. Mycenae was their greatest city, built on top of a low hill which rose from a flat, fertile plain. It was surrounded by walls of gigantic size.

With the fall of the Minoan civilization the Mycenaeans grew in strength and spread their power and influence over a wide area of the Mediterranean. The Mycenaeans learned the art of writing from the Minoans (see page 10) and their craftsmen made objects of great beauty from metal and stone. Mycenaean engineers built canals and reclaimed land from marshes; roads and bridges connected towns and architects designed palaces for their rulers – as at Mycenae, Tiryns and Thebes. They were traders and warriors, and were ruled over by kings.

Mycenae was excavated by the German archaeologist Heinrich Schliemann, in the 1870s. He discovered the tombs of the early kings of Mycenae. The dead kings, their faces covered with gold masks, had been buried with hundreds of

precious objects in deep shaft graves. In 1952 some more graves were found, just outside the city wall.

The Mycenaeans were the first true Greeks. Hundreds of years after the end of their civilization, Greek poets and storytellers remembered them as a race of heroes.

Heinrich Schliemann, the German archaeologist who excavated Mycenae.

Fact File

End of the Greek Bronze Age

The Mycenaean civilization was really quite short-lived, and after 300 years of prosperity it went into decline, starting about 1200 BC (3,200 years ago). This was a time of trouble and Mycenaean cities had walls built to defend them from attackers. The city wall around Mycenae was 900 metres long. Poor harvests caused famine and some Mycenaeans may have left Greece to start new lives elsewhere in the Mediterranean area. These times were so unsettling for the population that the art of writing was forgotten. The so-called Dark Ages had begun.

▲

This death mask of thin gold, 3,500 years old, was found by Schliemann in one of the kings' graves at Mycenae. It is known as the 'Mask of Agamemnon', a legendary king of Mycenae. The real name of the king it was made for is not known.

This was the main gate into Mycenae, built about 1250 BC. Because of the two lion-like animals carved above it, it is called the 'Lion Gate'. It is the oldest example of large-scale sculpture in Europe.

Sheets of bronze have been bent into shape to make this heavy suit of armour. It belonged to a Mycenaean soldier. He must have been an important man because armour such as this would have been expensive. The helmet was made from boars' tusks. Almost all we know about Mycenaean armour has been learned from this unique example.

THE WORLD OF THE GREEKS

Dark Age Greece: the time of Homer

Fact File

Troy – fact or fiction?

Schliemann believed Troy had really existed – but others said it was only a story made up by Homer. In the 1870s he excavated at Hissarlik (a place in Turkey) and correctly identified it as Troy – the city in the legend. In fact, there were several cities buried in the hill at Hissarlik, each one built on top of the ruins of another. It was a real jigsaw puzzle for an archaeologist! Schliemann dug through them all and we now know that the city he said was Troy was even older than the one described by Homer. Schliemann had dug straight through Homer's Troy without knowing it! In the city he dug down to, he found a great treasure of gold jewellery. For many years it was kept in the Berlin Museum in Germany, but it disappeared during World War II and is now known to be in Russia.

The Dark Ages were a time of great unrest and hardship. In a way, it was like switching a light off on the glory of the Bronze Age and forgetting that it had ever happened – and the darkness that fell over Greece lasted for about 300 years, from 1100 to 800 BC (3,100 to 2,800 years ago).

But what were the Dark Ages like? We know that the Minoan and Mycenaean civilizations came to a sudden end. But who was the enemy? The Ancient Egyptians said that about the year 1190 BC a great number of invaders were forced out of Egypt. They took to the sea and are known as the 'Sea Peoples'. It is possible that they sailed to Crete and then on to mainland Greece, destroying the societies they found there. A Mycenaean 'Linear B' writing tablet refers to men acting as look-outs along the coast.

For whatever reason the Dark Ages began, during this period there were no great advances in Greek civilization. The arts of writing and wall painting were abandoned, pottery had simple decoration only, buildings became simpler and trading contacts were temporarily broken. People lived modestly in country villages.

It was during the Dark Ages that poets composed long stories about ancient glories. They were passed on by word of mouth, from one generation to the next. One of the most famous poets was Homer and his two epic poems, the 'Iliad' and the 'Odyssey', still survive. When Heinrich Schliemann read the 'Iliad' he was so sure it was a true story that he set about uncovering the world of Homer's Greece. He tried to find the cities of Troy and Mycenae, both of which Homer had described.

Homer was one of the greatest Greek poets – but we know little about him. We think he lived at the end of the Dark Ages, possibly around 850 BC. He may have been born on the island of Chios. One story says he was blind. His poems, 'Iliad' and 'Odyssey', are about the Trojan War – a war fought by the Mycenaeans against the city of Troy, 400 years before Homer composed his poems.

The fall of Troy is described in Homer's 'Odyssey' poem. A Greek army built a gigantic wooden horse and left it outside the city of Troy. The Trojans thought it was a gift and took it into their city. At night, Greek soldiers hiding inside the horse climbed out and opened the city gates to let their army inside. A battle was fought and Troy was captured by the cunning Greeks.

A silver coin called a 'tetradrachm'. It was used at the Greek colony of Syracuse, Sicily, about 485 BC. The portrait is surrounded by dolphins, a common mammal in the Aegean Sea.

Archaic Greece: overseas colonies

After the Dark Ages ended, the Greeks enjoyed a period of prosperity. During the 200 years of the so-called Archaic Period (700 to 500 BC), many of the signs of civilization reappeared. Along with foreign trade, skills such as writing, painting, sculpture and large-scale building flourished. One of the most visible signs of renewed Greek activity was their expansion to new lands overseas, where they built Greek cities.

A map of the Greek world at this time shows how many colonies the Greeks founded. They stretched from Spain and France in the west to the coasts of Turkey and Syria in the east. The first were in Asia Minor and were settled by mainland Greeks from about 1000 BC. It was during the Archaic Period that most colonies were established. The last Greek colonies to be founded were on the coast of north Africa and around the Black Sea, in parts of

Several temples were built at the colony of Akragas (modern Agrigento) in southern Sicily. The colony was founded by Greeks from the island of Rhodes in 581 BC. This picture shows the temple of Concord – one of the best preserved of all Greek temples. It has survived in good condition because it was later used as a church and was not allowed to fall to ruin.

present-day Romania and Georgia.

The Greeks went overseas because of poverty at home and because they wanted to increase trade. As Greek cities began to prosper once more, the population increased and farmers could not produce enough food for all to eat. It was then that people first thought about emigrating in order to make new lives for themselves.

All colonies had a 'parent city' in Greece. Colonies were the 'children' of the parent city. The parent city would organize and pay for a new colony to be founded.

This map shows how far the Greeks travelled in search of new land to colonize. Note how they settled close to the sea which was their route back to Greece. They rarely ventured inland because to do so meant coming into contact with people who may have been hostile to them. Also, places where there were already successful civilizations, as in Egypt, were considered out of bounds. An exception was at Naukratis, where the colony acted as an important trading centre between Greece and Egypt. There were so many Greek colonies in southern Italy and Sicily that this area has been called 'Magna Graecia' which means 'Greater Greece'.

Fact File

Table of Greek colonies

Hundreds of colonies were founded during the years of Greek expansion. Many of them became successful cities in their own right and some modern towns and villages can trace their history back to the Greek colonies of over 2,500 years ago. Here is a table of ten such places from west to east on the map below.

	Greek name	Modern name	Country
1.	Malaca	Malaga	Spain
2.	Massalia	Marseille	France
3.	Caralis	Cagliari	Sardinia
4.	Neapolis	Naples	Italy
5.	Syracuse	Syracuse	Sicily
6.	Apollonia	Pojan	Albania
7.	Byzantion	Istanbul	Turkey
8.	Odessos	Odessa	Ukraine
9.	Naukratis	El Nibeira	Egypt
10.	Euesperides	Benghazi	Libya

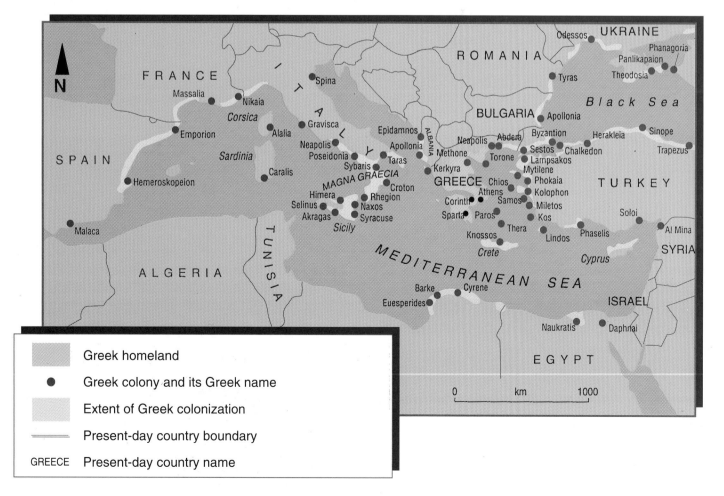

Greek homeland

● Greek colony and its Greek name

Extent of Greek colonization

Present-day country boundary

GREECE Present-day country name

Athens, Sparta and city-states

Democracy in action. This is a special piece of broken pottery called an 'ostracon'. On it is scratched the name of a politician, 'Hippokrates the Alkmeonid', whom the voters wanted to be ostracized (sent away). If enough people voted this way, Hippokrates would have to leave politics and Athens for ten years!

These are the Taygetos mountains, rising to 2,400 metres and capped with snow until late spring. It was here that Spartan babies and children were sent if they seemed weak or sickly – the Spartan state only wanted the fittest to survive.

While some Greeks were busy sailing off to start new lives abroad, others stayed at home and built up their home cities into what we call 'city-states'. The two best known city-states were Athens and Sparta.

Because Greece is a mountainous country, it was possible for groups of Greeks to form their own self-governing independent states within valleys or on plains. Each city-state had one main city, usually walled, and land to govern, in which most of the citizens worked. If the city-state controlled colonies abroad, then it could grow rich and strong from the taxes sent back to it.

The Greeks used the word 'polis' to describe a city-state. Do you recognize this word at all? You should! You use it, or at least something like it, every time you say 'police' or 'political' – just two of our own words that can be traced back to the Greeks!

The largest city-state was Athens. It had a lot of land (about 2,500 square kilometres), owned valuable silver mines, and had its own port (at Piraeus). After a war against the Persians (see page 22) the Athenians built a great defensive wall right around the city and port. Within the city was a large flat-topped rock called the 'Acropolis', where the early Athenians had lived during the Archaic Period. When the population increased in numbers

they moved down the hill and built their first proper city on the flat area beneath it. The Acropolis remained important and in later years many fine temples were built on it (see page 32).

Sparta was very different from Athens. Its city lay in a plain on the Peloponnese and the state was noted for the strict treatment of its people. The warlike Spartans, both men and women, were subjected to rigorous training programmes designed to enforce obedience and improve strength. Spartan soldiers were some of the strongest and best trained in the Greek world. Fearing no one, their city was un-walled, and as the Spartan leader Lycurgus put it, 'It is men, not walls, that make a city'.

These are laws of the city-state of Gortyn, a city on the island of Crete. They were carved into the wall of a theatre about 450 BC, though they would have been used for a long time before this date. Different states had their own laws, each proclaiming their particular form of government and social structure.

A bronze figure of a young Spartan girl. Her short skirt tells us she was from Sparta, as all other Greek women wore long dresses. This girl is running barefoot – another sign she was from the tough Spartan city-state.

Classical Greece: the 'Golden Age'

The years 500 to 323 BC (2,500 to 2,323 years ago) marked the Classical Period, and nowhere is it better seen than in Athens. Under the great Athenian leader, Pericles, beautiful temples were built on top of the Acropolis (see page 32) and art, science, philosophy and politics flourished. Athens grew rich and emerged as the most important of all the Greek cities, controlling the whole of the Aegean and much of the mainland. Her port, at Piraeus, became the largest in the Greek world, and her navy the strongest.

During the 400s BC as many as 200,000 people are thought to have lived in Athens and the surrounding countryside. The city attracted people from all over the Greek world. Craftworkers, merchants, business people, artists and poets came to Athens to live and work. It was a 'Golden Age', when Pericles said that Athens was the 'greatest name in history…a power to be remembered forever'. He spoke the truth, because much of what the Athenians enjoyed 2,500 years ago forms the cornerstone of our own society. For example, many aspects of theatre, architecture, sculpture, philosophy and democracy were developed by the Greeks during their Golden Age, and have been handed down to us today.

◀ The Athenian leader Pericles. He was responsible for building the Acropolis temples.

A warship from the Athenian navy.

Temples on the Acropolis at Athens.

This is how the Acropolis at Athens looked in about 425 BC (2,425 years ago). The largest temple, called the Parthenon, stood on the highest part of the flat-topped hill and smaller temples were built lower down. The city of Athens was built on the flat area below the Acropolis. Travellers approaching Athens would have seen the Acropolis temples from far away, and their sheer size and number proclaimed to the world how wealthy Athens was during the 'Golden Age'.

Fact File

The rise of Macedonia

The 'Golden Age' at Athens could not last for ever. A bitter war broke out between Athens and Sparta (known as the Peloponnesian War) and lasted for 27 years. In 404 BC Athens surrendered to Sparta and the great days of Athens came to an end. Democracy was abolished and was replaced by an unpopular 'oligarchy', which meant rule by a few wealthy people. With the decline of Athens and later of Sparta, wars broke out between other cities, each trying to fill the power gap. But while these cities quarrelled they were distracted from what was happening in Macedonia – a region in the north-east of the mainland where local chieftains had become powerful kings. Under the Macedonian king, Philip II, and then his son Alexander, weakened Greek cities were defeated by Macedonian armies. In 338 BC Philip took control of the whole of the Greek mainland.

A silver coin with a portrait of Alexander the Great.

Alexander's empire and the route he took on his ten year trail of conquests. This was the extent of his empire at the time of his death in 323 BC. He established Greek cities throughout his empire, and at least 13 were named after him. Bucephala, in India, was named after Alexander's favourite horse, Bucephalus. On a modern map, Alexander's empire would take in all or part of 17 countries.

Macedonian Greece: Philip and Alexander

Macedonia is a region in the north of Greece. It has lakes, flood plains that are cultivated for farming and a changeable climate.

Macedonia was ruled by a royal family. Its kings were warriors in charge of a powerful and well organized army. To the south of Macedonia the Peloponnesian War (see page 21) had left the Greek city-states damaged and weak. King Philip realized this was his chance to expand his Macedonian empire. In 338 BC he won a decisive battle at Chaeronea bringing the Greek states under his control. But Philip did not live long to enjoy his success; he was murdered two years after his great victory.

Philip's young son, Alexander, inherited his father's new kingdom. He was just 20 years old – too young to be in charge his critics said. But Alexander proved them wrong. Not only did he keep his Greek kingdom together but he also invaded the powerful empire of Darius III. His empire centred on Persia (modern Iran) and his capital was at Susa. Alexander's army won many battles, marching nearly 20,000 kilometres on their campaign. When he died, at the age of only 33, Alexander's army had conquered most of the world known to the Ancient Greeks. His empire stretched from Asia Minor (modern Turkey) in the west, to India in the east. Because of his achievements he became known as 'Alexander the Great'.

The Empire of Alexander the Great

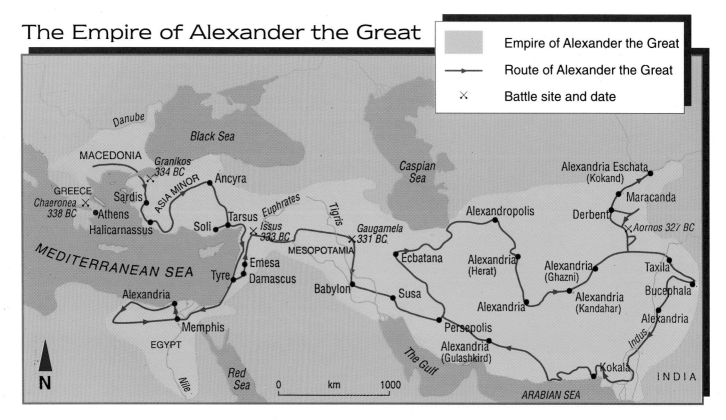

The Hellenistic Period

Alexander the Great died in Babylon in 323 BC and was buried at Alexandria in Egypt. His wife, Roxane, and their young child were murdered in the bitter struggle for power between his generals that followed his death. His massive empire gradually fell apart and some of his generals set themselves up as kings in Egypt, Asia and Greece. They observed Greek customs and erected Greek-style buildings. This was the time of the Hellenistic kingdoms (from the Greek 'Hellenistes' meaning 'imitators of the Greeks'). The Hellenistic Period lasted for about 300 years, until its kingdoms were swallowed up by the expanding Roman Empire.

▲ A Roman mosaic from Pompeii, Italy. It shows Alexander riding his horse, Bucephalus, at the battle of Issus, where the Persian king Darius III was defeated. Alexander is to the left and Darius is in the centre, in a chariot.

This model shows how Philip II may have ▶ looked. It is based on fragments of the skull from the gold casket found in the Macedonian royal tomb at Vergina. Note the damage to the right eye. Philip was wounded in the right eye during a siege and a scar like this would have been left.

In 1977 archaeologists discovered the tomb of a Macedonian king at Vergina in northern Greece. It was probably the tomb of Philip II and this gold casket held his cremated remains. The star on the lid is a symbol of the Macedonian royal family.

ACHIEVEMENTS OF THE GREEKS

Writing and the alphabet

An inscription carefully carved in capital letters on an altar at Sparta. Compare the letters to those shown in the illustration opposite. Can you work out what some of them are?

Wherever you travel in Ancient Greece you will see inscriptions, such as ones carved into walls, as at Gortyn (see page 19), on the bases of statues, and even scratched on to pieces of pottery (see page 18). Some Greek letters can be recognized straight away because we use the same ones in our own alphabet. But others are unfamiliar and at first sight make no sense to us. Because the letters were mostly straight lines, with no awkward curves, they were easy to chisel into stone.

The Greeks borrowed their alphabet from the Phoenicians, who lived in the Middle East, in what is now Lebanon, Jordan, Syria and Israel. The Phoenicians invented a form of writing about 1000 BC (3,000 years ago) and it was these so-called 'foreign marks' that the Greeks adapted when they rediscovered the art of writing. Their own 'Linear B' writing system (see page 11) had been lost with the destruction of the palaces at the end of the Bronze Age, about 1200 BC (3,200 years ago).

The first Greek alphabet was made about 700 BC, at the start of the Archaic Period (see page 16). At first it looked very like the Phoenician alphabet and inscriptions written in it read from right to left – a style copied from the Phoenicians. But within 200 years the Greeks changed the direction and from then on writing left to right became the normal style. They added new signs to represent vowel sounds not present in the Phoenician script and by 500 BC the Greek alphabet had reached its final form.

An inscription on a bronze tablet. It refers to an agreement made between two Greek cities Oeantheia and Chaleion.

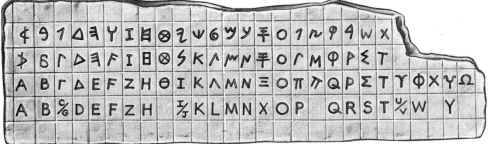

1000 BC PHOENICIAN ALPHABET

700 BC ARCHAIC GREEK ALPHABET

500 BC CLASSICAL GREEK ALPHABET

MODERN ALPHABET

The Classical Greek alphabet, in use from about 500 BC, compared to Archaic Greek and Phoenician alphabets. The word 'alphabet' comes from the first two letters of the Greek alphabet, 'alpha' and 'beta'.

Fact File

Papyrus, parchment and stone

Much of what we know about Ancient Greece comes from reading inscriptions the Greeks carved in stone. Even ancient graffiti can be useful! Sometimes this can tell us more than official writings, which after a while start to follow a set pattern and tell us very little. But other than stone, what else did the Greeks write on? They would certainly have written on papyrus (a kind of paper made from reeds), brought to Greece from Egypt. Parchment (specially prepared sheepskin or goatskin) was also used.

An inscription on a block of marble. It refers to a woman called Tertia and was an offering to the god Zeus. She may have had something wrong with her face which she hoped Zeus would cure. Can you tell which word is her name? The alphabet above will help.

Science, medicine and learning

The work of Greek architects and sculptors is everywhere to be seen – we only have to visit a ruined city or go to a museum to see evidence of their skilful work. But there is much more to the Greek world than old stones. There is also the legacy of the Greek scientists, doctors and thinkers whose work added to the greatness of Greek society.

Who's who in science?

Archimedes: One of the greatest mathematicians and engineers of the ancient world. He came from the Greek colony of Syracuse, in Sicily. One of his studies involved measuring volumes of objects. He measured how much water overflowed from his bath when he got into it, and from this he discovered that a solid object always displaces its own volume of water.

Eratosthenes: He was one of the cleverest men of the ancient world, with interests in astronomy, geography, mathematics and philosophy. He worked out that the world was round and not flat – a fact that was eventually forgotten and then 'rediscovered' in Europe in the 16th century AD, 1,700 years after Eratosthenes had first said it!

The mathematician Archimedes was murdered by a Roman soldier in Syracuse, his home town, in 212 BC, as seen in this mosaic.

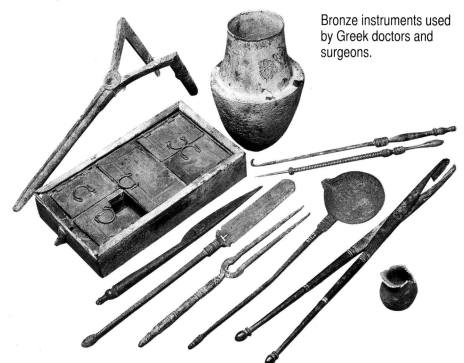
Bronze instruments used by Greek doctors and surgeons.

Fact File

A Greek calculator?

When a large lump of bronze was found on a ship wrecked off the Dodecanese island of Anticythera, archaeologists had trouble deciding what it had been. Inside the lump were at least 20 gear wheels originally mounted inside a wooden box, some with instructions written on them. It was a baffling puzzle. To an astronomer such as Eratosthenes (see left) it would have been the very latest piece of scientific equipment. We now know it was a calculator for plotting the movements of the sun, moon and stars, made in about 100 BC.

The ancient calculator from Anticythera.

Who's who in medicine?

Hippocrates: A doctor from the island of Kos where he founded an important medical centre. He worked closely with his patients and learned about their ailments from careful observations. Before Hippocrates, people relied on magic and superstition. His approach was what we would call scientific. Other doctors visited him and learned about medicine from him. They spread his knowledge and medical techniques throughout the Greek world. Hippocrates believed in practical cures that could be proved to work rather than in cures that relied on magic.

Who's who in learning?

Socrates: A philosopher from Athens. In his teachings he pointed to weaknesses in government. He taught people to think for themselves and encouraged his students to do the same. This was seen as corrupting youth, for which he stood trial. He was condemned to death and died after taking poison.

Plato: He had ideas on how to make a perfect state which he explained in his influential writings. In Athens he founded a school for thinking and reasoning which became famous throughout the ancient world. People studied there for hundreds of years, until it was closed by the Christian emperor Justinian, in AD 529.

A marble bust of Plato. His important teachings continue to influence governments to this day.

27

Theatre and music

Two female musicians. They are playing a flute and a lyre.

The lives of the Greeks were enriched by their love of music and theatre. Most towns had an open-air theatre where plays were performed. They were put on during the daytime, not at night. Actors spoke or sang their parts from a circular stage area of beaten earth called the 'orchestra'.

The audience sat on stone seats around the orchestra. The seats were uncomfortable, so people brought cushions to sit on. Everyone had a clear view of the proceedings, and the actors' voices could be heard from all parts of the theatre, even by people sitting on the back row.

All the parts in a Greek play were played by male actors. They wore thick-soled shoes, tall wigs and padded clothes to make them look larger and more visible to the people sitting a long way from the stage. Happy characters dressed in brightly-coloured clothes; criminals and unlucky characters wore grey, green or blue clothes

The theatre at Epidavros could seat 12,000 people. It is still used today for performances during the summer.

What did they wear?

We know about Greek clothes from pictures on pottery and, of course, from statues. Both men and women wore loose fitting clothes made from wool or linen. Women wore a dress called a 'chiton' which was a one-piece tunic wrapped around the body and left open down one side. It was fastened at the shoulder with pins, some of which were quite ornate. In the Classical Period women's dresses were decorated with coloured patterns and some had gold ornaments sewn on to them. At this time women wore their hair up and it was held in place with ribbons or scarves.

Men's clothes were simpler. They wore tunics, either long or short, fastened at the shoulder. Both men and women wore leather sandals.

Clay masks worn by actors. They were designed to portray the character and feelings of the person the actor was playing. All masks had large gaping mouths which helped to increase the size of the actor's voice and project it to the back of the theatre. Wigs and false beards were attached to the masks.

and those in mourning wore black. Gods and goddesses were distinguished by their wands and tridents and hunters always had a purple shawl around their left arm. Masks played an important part in the theatre and were meant to exaggerate the actor's character. By changing masks the actor could change from one character to another. The audience would have understood all these strict conventions.

Music was important in the lives of the Ancient Greeks, and they used many different kinds of musical instruments. Woodwind instruments included several kinds of pipes, and lyres and harps were their stringed instruments. We know about Greek instruments from pictures painted on their pottery.

The scene on this vase shows how Greek women dressed in about 450 BC, wearing fashionable one-piece 'chitons' or tunics. The girl sitting down is being prepared for her wedding by an attendant, who is bringing a necklace to her. A mirror hangs on the wall.

Army, navy and fighting

When it came to fighting, the Greeks could raise formidable armies and navies. Warfare was an ever-present part of Greek life, and for some Greeks, such as the Spartans, being able to fight was part of growing up. The earliest references to Greek armies are in the epic poems of Homer, where he describes Bronze Age armies attacking cities such as Troy (see page 14). Greek city-states often fought each other, as Athens and Sparta did in the Peloponnesian War (see page 20). By the time of Alexander the Great military tactics had reached their strongest point, enabling him to win a massive empire in about ten years of fighting (see page 22).

The army

Armies of the Archaic Period relied on fast-moving cavalry, but by the Classical Period the foot soldier had become more important. Foot soldiers fought in the armies of the city-states. They wore bronze armour consisting of a helmet, a breastplate and leg-guards (called 'greaves'). Each soldier carried a heavy shield, a sword (usually made of iron) and a spear which was up to three metres long. The army of Alexander the Great was made of thousands of well-trained soldiers and non-Greek mercenaries (soldiers who fought for money rather than for a cause which they believed in). Alexander's soldiers marched into battle in a closed formation called a 'phalanx'. This was like a human battering ram that advanced with hundreds of long spears pointing at the enemy. Within the army was an elite class of soldiers called 'hoplites'. They were soldiers who could afford the best armour. For some soldiers armour would have been a nuisance. For example, archers wore little armour because they had to be free to move quickly.

A bronze helmet worn by a soldier in about 450 BC. Soldiers from different regions of Greece wore different styles of helmet.

Fact File

Battle of Marathon

What does the word 'Marathon' make you think of? You might think of super-fit athletes running a long race in under two hours – or flabby joggers struggling to do it in more than twice that time! But where does the word 'Marathon' come from? In 490 BC a Persian army landed on the mainland of Greece and a battle was fought on the plain of Marathon, near Athens. About 9,000 Athenians faced a much larger Persian army. Against all the odds they won, with the loss of only 192 men. A runner was sent from the battlefield to Athens with news of the victory. The distance from Marathon to Athens was just under 50 kilometres, and the messenger ran all the way. This is how the length of the modern Marathon race originated.

Soldiers in battle, painted on a vase of about 500 BC. Note their helmets, shields and spears.

A trireme battleship and a merchant ship painted on a vase of about 540 BC. The merchant ship was powered by sail alone, whereas the trireme had oars and a sail.

The navy

The supreme fighting ship of the Athenian navy was the trireme. It was a wooden battleship powered by 170 oarsmen arranged in three levels on each side. A trireme would disable an enemy ship by ramming it at speed, punching a hole in the side with its long nose, or prow, which was reinforced with bronze.

Breaking the oars of a ship was another tactic used to disable enemy vessels. In the famous sea battle at Salamis in 480 BC, the Athenian navy destroyed 200 ships of the Persian navy.

This modern copy of a trireme was made in 1987 and can be seen sailing in the Aegean. On Ancient Greek triremes, large eyes painted on the prow were intended to frighten the enemy.

Temples and columns

This temple stands near the Parthenon and is called the Erechtheum. Instead of columns it has six female figures called 'Caryatids'. Cleverly, the drapes of their dresses have been carved to resemble column flutes.

An important part of many Greek towns was a high hill, known as an 'acropolis'. This is a Greek word which means 'upper city'. It was where the town's inhabitants sheltered in times of trouble, as well as being a place where temples were built.

The most famous Greek acropolis is at Athens, where the hill rises 100 metres above the lower town. On the hill's flat top stands a group of temples, the greatest of which is the Parthenon.

This fine building was begun in 447 BC, on the orders of the Athenian statesman Pericles (see page 20) to celebrate the start of a time of peace after the war against Persia ended in victory for the Greeks.

The Parthenon is named after the goddess Athena Parthenos, in whose honour the temple was built. Inside stood a giant statue of Athena, about 12 metres tall, parts of which were made of gold and ivory.

Each year the Panathenaia festival (this means 'All Athenian') was held to honour Athena, when pilgrims walked in a procession to the Parthenon. Once every four years a tunic was draped over her statue, where it remained for the next four years. The placing of the gown on the figure was

The Parthenon in Athens is the most famous of all Greek temples. It is 70 metres long and has 56 Doric columns. The temple was built from the finest white marble which was originally painted in bright colours.

the most solemn part of the festival, after which cows were sacrificed at the altar. The cooked meat was taken back down to the city and shared amongst the people.

Part of the frieze from the Parthenon. It shows 192 horsemen and may commemorate the men who died in the battle of Marathon (see page 30). Many of these famous stones are now in the British Museum, London, where they are known as the 'Elgin Marbles' – after Lord Elgin who brought them to Britain in the 1800s. Many Greeks would like to see them returned to Greece.

The three main types of column

Doric columns
were the earliest and simplest and were used in the Parthenon. The tops were plain.

Ionic columns
were thinner and had slightly decorated tops. They also had bases.

Corinthian columns
had elaborate tops decorated with acanthus leaves, a plant with spiny leaves.

Fact File

Tricks with columns

Look closely at these three views of the front of the Parthenon.

This is how the Parthenon appears to us, with perfectly horizontal and vertical lines.

This is how it would appear if it was built with lines which really were perfectly horizontal and vertical.

This is how the Greeks actually built it – with inward leaning columns! They knew that horizontal lines appear to curve in the middle and vertical lines appear to fall outwards. You can test this last point by looking up at a tall building. Several optical illusions were built into the Parthenon to make it look 'right'. The inward lean is so slight that the columns would have to be 1,500 metres tall before they touched! Two-fifths of the way up the columns swell out slightly – this stops them from looking thin in the middle. The bulge is called an 'entasis'.

Statues and pottery

Most Greek figures made from bronze were melted down long ago. This one, possibly of the god Zeus, has survived because it was lost at sea until modern fishermen caught it in their nets. A bronze lightening bolt was held in the right hand. Some experts think it is a statue of the god Poseidon. If so, he may have held a trident in his hand. It was made about 470 BC.

The Ancient Greeks were master craftspeople and they made wonderful stone and bronze statues. Some of the oldest examples of human figures made in Greece are the 4,500-year-old ones from the Cyclades Islands (see page 8). However, there's no resemblance between these strange little Bronze Age figures and the statues made in the Archaic and Classical Periods, some 2,000 years later.

The best collection of statues in Greece is in the National Archaeological Museum in Athens, where hundreds have been brought together from all over the country. The earliest statues are called 'kouroi', if they are male, and 'korai' if they are female ('kouros' and 'kore' are the words for single statues). These names are from a Greek word meaning 'youths' because the statues usually show young men and women. Many were made on the island of Naxos. They are life-size or taller, usually of white marble and were originally painted. Statues of this kind were made over a period of 200 years, from 650 BC to 450 BC. They probably served as grave markers, like headstones, or as memorials set up outside temples. These early statues show how their sculptors grew more confident as they learned more about working with marble.

By the Classical Period life-like studies of gods, athletes, statesmen, ordinary people and animals were being made in workshops all over Greece. Their statues were life-like studies and

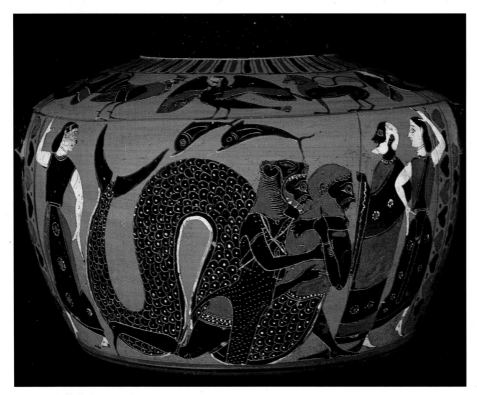

A black-figure vase showing the hero Heracles fighting the fish-tailed sea god Triton. This vase was made in Athens about 550 BC.

A red-figure vase showing a small child in a potty chair, holding a rattle.

showed great attention to detail, unlike the older 'kouroi' and 'korai' which were heavy-handed by comparison. Statues of this period were made to decorate public and private buildings and were carved from marble or cast in bronze. Both stone and metal statues were painted in vivid colours, so they could be seen from a distance. Today the paint on most of them has worn away.

Fact File

Painted pottery

The painted pottery of the Greeks is some of the most skilful ever made. Many different painting styles were used, on lots of different shapes of pot. One particular style is called black-figure pottery, where red pots were painted with little black figures. This style was popular from about 600 BC to 480 BC. Another type of pottery was red-figure pottery. This was popular from about 530 BC to 350 BC and was where black pots were decorated with figures in red. Both types were made in Athens, the most famous centre for pottery making for over 200 years. Painters created wonderful works of art. They treated the surface of pots as artists today would use canvas, covering them with scenes of gods, battles, games and everyday life.

This polished marble figure was made by the master sculptor Praxiteles about 350 BC. It shows the god Hermes holding the baby Dionysus. The baby is reaching out for something held by Hermes, possibly a bunch of grapes (now missing along with his right arm). Note how the figure leans against a tree stump for support – it would not have been able to stand otherwise.

A youthful 'kouros' marble figure made about 600 BC. His pose is typical – straight arms, clenched fists, legs slightly astride and braided hair. All 'kouroi' have a distinctive little smile which makes them look happy!

A 'kore' marble figure made about 600 BC. Female figures were always shown clothed, whereas male figures were naked.

RELIGION AND FESTIVALS

Gods and goddesses

The Charioteer of Delphi. It was part of a group given by the ruler of Syracuse, Sicily, to the gods as thanks for his wins at the games at Olympia. The statue dates from about 475 BC.

In the Greek religion there were many gods and goddesses, each of whom performed a different duty. The most important gods were the Olympians – six gods and six goddesses – who were often simply referred to as 'the Twelve' (see table opposite). People believed they lived on Mount Olympus, which is the highest mountain in Greece (2917 metres high).

Many other lesser gods and spirits (called nymphs) were worshipped too, especially those associated with nature. Nymphs were shy, secretive creatures who represented the beauty of nature. The Naiads were nymphs of streams, and the Dryads were nymphs of trees.

A Greek proverb said: 'Gifts persuade the gods'. The greatest gift a person could give the gods was an animal. A sheep was the usual offering – but an ox pleased the gods more because it was a gift of great value. Animals were sacrificed outside temples, and their meat was burnt on a fire. The smoke drifted up into the sky, and into the realm of the gods.

If an animal was not sacrificed, gifts of food, clothing, locks of hair, or pieces of pottery were left on the gods' altars. But no matter how great or simple an offering was, they all had one thing in common – the wish to please the gods in return for their protection. People asked them to protect their town, their homes, their fields, and their families.

Poseidon
He carried a trident – a three-pronged spear. The Greeks believed he created the first horse.

Aphrodite
Because the Greeks believed she was born from the foam of the sea, she was shown floating on it.

The twelve Olympian gods

Aphrodite	goddess of love and beauty.
Apollo	god of sun, light and good fortune.
Ares	god of war.
Artemis	goddess of hunting and protector of girls.
Athena	goddess of wisdom, art and war.
Demeter	goddess of produce, especially grain.
Hephaestus	god of fire and blacksmiths.
Hera	goddess of marriage and women.
Hermes	god of the countryside, protector of travellers and messenger of the gods.
Hestia	goddess of the family and the hearth.
Poseidon	god of the sea, earthquakes, horses and bulls.
Zeus	god of the sky and all other gods.

Fact File

The Oracle at Delphi

Ancient Greeks even had their own version of horoscopes and Delphi was the place to go to learn what the future held in store. According to legend, vapours came from a crack in the ground and anyone who breathed them in could predict the future. A temple to the god Apollo was built over the crack and three priestesses, called the 'Pythia', then became the only people allowed to make predictions. At first they made predictions only once a year, but later it became once a month for nine months of the year. They spoke in a strange language and their male assistants interpreted it. Alexander the Great is supposed to have visited Delphi and was told, 'My son, none can resist thee'. He went on to win a great empire (see page 22). More ordinary people were given advice about their health, their families or their businesses. The Oracle survived into Christian times until it was abolished by the Romans in AD 385.

Zeus
The supreme god. He was said to have created all the people in the world, giving them happy or unhappy characters which he took from two jars. Zeus was also thought to control the weather, especially storms and is shown holding a lightning bolt.

Athena
Her helmet, shield and spear are signs of her war-like nature. The owl at her feet shows her wisdom and love of art. Athens was named after her.

Myths and legends

The Ancient Greeks told stories about heroes, gods, adventures, wars and treasures. The stories helped them to understand the world in which they lived. Stories grew longer and more detailed the more they were told. We call these stories about legendary people and places 'myths'.

Storytellers recited stories and poems at public meetings. To make them interesting to listen to, they spoke or sang in a flowing musical rhythm.

A popular series of stories was about the Trojan War which ended with the building of a great wooden horse (see page 15). The vivid character of the Greek and Trojan heroes, and the gods and goddesses who fought alongside them, entertained their listeners on many a long evening.

In other stories human weaknesses were used to make moral points as in the story of Daedalus and his son, Icarus. The young Icarus went against his father's advice and flew too close to the sun. The wax holding his wings together melted and Icarus fell to his death. An Aegean island is named after him (Ikaria), probably because it is wing-shaped.

A painting of Theseus killing the Minotaur. Painted on a vase of about 450 BC.

Siren

Gorgon

Pegasus

Hydra

The Labyrinth

A well-known myth is the story of Theseus and the Minotaur, a monster that lived in a maze on the island of Crete. The maze was called the Labyrinth. It was so complicated that no one who entered it could ever hope to find their way out. Fourteen young people from Athens were fed to the Minotaur every nine years. Theseus set out to kill it. He was helped by Ariadne who had fallen in love with him. She gave him a ball of wool, which he unwound as he walked through the maze. After killing the Minotaur, Theseus found his way out of the maze by following the wool back to the entrance. Did the Labyrinth really exist? Some people think the palace of Knossos (see page 10) was the setting for the story, as it had as many as 1,000 inter-connecting rooms.

Minotaur

Ten figures from the Trojan War

Greeks

1. Achilles — the greatest Greek hero, famous for his strength and courage. He killed the Trojan warrior, Hector.
2. Agamemnon — the king of Mycenae and leader of the Greek forces against the Trojans.
3. Helen — the beautiful daughter of Zeus who eloped with the Trojan, Paris.
4. Menelaus — Agamemnon's brother and husband of Helen. The Trojan War began when Helen deserted Menelaus and fled to Troy.
5. Nestor — the oldest and most experienced of the Greek chieftains, renowned for his mature wisdom.
6. Odysseus — a Greek chieftain whose plan it was to build the wooden horse that tricked the Trojans (see page 15).

Trojans

7. Aeneas — a Trojan hero who was a match for the Greek hero Achilles.
8. Hector — leader of the Trojan forces who held out against the Greeks for ten years until slain by Achilles.
9. Paris — the abductor of Helen and because of this the Trojan War began. He killed the Greek hero Achilles.
10. Priam — the King of Troy and father of Hector. He was tricked by the Greeks and let their wooden horse enter his city.

Ten creatures in Greek myths

1. Centaur — a wild creature, half man, half horse.
2. Cyclops — a one-eyed giant who ate people.
3. Gorgon — a female monster with live snakes for hair, whose stare turned people to stone.
4. Harpy — a flesh-eating flying monster, with a woman's face and bird's wings and claws.
5. Hydra — a huge snake with many heads; if one was cut off, two grew in its place.
6. Minotaur — a monster imprisoned in the Labyrinth, with a man's body and a bull's head.
7. Pegasus — a beautiful white, flying horse.
8. Satyr — a playful young goat-like being, spirit of woods and hills.
9. Siren — a sea-dwelling female with a lovely singing voice, who lured sailors to their deaths on rocks.
10. Sphinx — a winged monster with a woman's head and a lion's body.

The Olympic Games

To the west of the Peloponnese is Olympia. It is famous throughout the world as the birthplace of the Olympic Games, which the Greeks held every four years in honour of the god Zeus. People believed that sport and religion were connected, and for this reason festivals often mixed the two together. The first Olympic Games were held in 776 BC.

Olympia was a meeting-place, where men from cities throughout the Greek world gathered to compete in the festival games, or join in as spectators. Women were barred from entering Olympia while the games were on.

Before the start of the games the Olympic Truce was declared. All fighting between cities was stopped until the end of the festival. People who went to the games went to Olympia in peace.

The contests at the Olympic Games were for men only. Athletes arrived at Olympia one month before the festival began. During this time they trained hard for their events. The games were held

The stadium at Olympia, where 40,000 spectators watched the finest athletes in the Greek world. Unlike our modern round tracks, the original Greek tracks were straight and athletes ran several lengths, depending on the type of race. This track was 190 metres long. Athletes entered the stadium through the short passageway, seen here.

A marble statue of a discus thrower. In most games male athletes competed naked, or nearly so.

The starting line for races inside the stadium at Olympia.

in August or September, and lasted for five days from the 12th to the 16th day of the month.

Winning athletes were awarded a garland of olive leaves and a palm frond, and ribbons were tied to their upper arms. A winning athlete was hailed as a hero who brought honour to his home town.

Besides the Olympic Games, other sporting festivals were the Pythian, Isthmian and Nemean Games. Collectively, these four festivals are known as the 'Panhellenic Games'.

In AD 393 the Romans stopped the Olympic Games because they wanted to abolish all pagan festivals. By that time the games had been held at Olympia for more than 1,100 years.

Athletes running in armour. Note their helmets, shields and leg armour.

Fact File

Olympic events

We're used to seeing many different sports in the modern Olympic Games. There were far fewer sports in the original games, and fewer competitors. Some events we still follow today, but others have not been revived. Here are the main events the Ancient Greeks competed in.

Boxing	*two men punched each other until one gave in or was knocked out. Hats were often worn for protection.*
Chariot racing	*chariots drawn by teams of horses raced around a circuit.*
Discus	*a polished flat disc of stone or metal was thrown as far as possible.*
Horse racing	*a long race in which the rider rode without a saddle.*
Javelin	*a pointed rod was thrown as far as possible.*
Jumping	*competitors jumped as far as they could from a standing start.*
Pentathlon	*a competition designed to find the best all-round athlete across five events: discus, javelin, jumping, running and wrestling ('penta' means 'five').*
Running	*the shortest race was the 'stade' which was one length of the track. The 'dolichos' race was ten lengths and the race in armour was two.*
Wrestling	*two men pushed and pulled each other until one gave in. A violent game, though killing one's opponent was strictly against the rules!*

Two men boxing, painted on a vase about 525 BC. On their hands are leather gloves.

THE END OF ANCIENT GREECE

The Greeks used tiny pieces of coloured stone to make pictures. But it was the Romans who produced the finest pictures, which we call 'mosaics'. This Roman mosaic has a Greek inscription.

Greece under the Romans

In the 3rd century BC the Romans, based in Italy, organized themselves and grew stronger. They could see the Greek world was splitting up after the death of Alexander the Great. This was their opportunity to expand beyond their own country, and one by one the Hellenistic kingdoms (successors to Alexander's empire – see page 23) came under Roman rule.

The Greek colonists in southern Italy and Sicily were the first to feel the new power of Rome and in 275 BC they were defeated by a Roman army. This was only the start of the Roman domination of the Greek world. In 146 BC Greece itself came under Roman rule and when Egypt became a Roman province in 30 BC the world of the Greeks was over.

The Romans learned many things from the Greeks. Greek statues were collected and taken back to Italy to adorn the rising capital of Rome. Roman craftspeople made copies of Greek bronze and marble figures, Roman buildings adopted Greek styles of architecture and even the Greek gods were taken over by the Romans who changed only their names.

Ephesus, a Greek city in Asia Minor (modern Turkey) was rebuilt and extended by the Romans. This is the Temple of Hadrian, built by the Romans about AD 150.

Roads at Ephesus were lined with rows of columns.

In many ways the Greek world never really disappeared because the Romans kept so many parts of it alive. The language the Romans used was Latin, not Greek. The Romans based their alphabet on the one used by the Greeks, and in turn this has become the one we use today.

New gods for old

The Romans matched the Greek gods with their own gods, and claimed them as their own. Here are the twelve Olympian gods worshipped by the Greeks, together with their 'new' Roman names.

Greek name	Roman name
Aphrodite	Venus
Apollo	Apollo
Ares	Mars
Artemis	Diana
Athena	Minerva
Demeter	Ceres
Hephaestus	Vulcan
Hera	Juno
Hermes	Mercury
Hestia	Vesta
Poseidon	Neptune
Zeus	Jupiter

(See page 37 to find out about the Greek gods.)

The Roman theatre at Ephesus could seat 24,000 spectators. Compare it with the picture of the Greek theatre on page 28.

Discovering Ancient Greece

The study of Ancient Greece began in earnest in the 1700s when wealthy Europeans made large collections of statues and pottery. It was considered fashionable to visit Greece and return with an 'antique'. Gradually, many of these objects found their way into museums around the world.

In the 1800s the first proper excavations were made in Greece. By then the aim was to discover the history of places and not just to look for long-lost works of art. Heinrich Schliemann's work at Mycenae is one of the best-known excavations of the 19th century (see page 12).

The 20th century saw great advances in understanding the Ancient Greeks, especially since we are now lucky enough to be able to work under water on ancient shipwrecks. A whole new world is open for the study of the Ancient Greeks, and archaeologists will be kept busy far into the future.

A modern excavation in progress. String divides the site into squares for the archaeologists to excavate. The soil is sieved so that nothing is missed, photographs are taken and detailed drawings are made. It is a long, slow process. Work on a major site goes on over many years, with teams of people from all over the world.

Treasure from the sea

Thousands of Ancient Greek ships must have been lost at sea. This now means big business for archaeologists and for treasure hunters. While archaeologists take several seasons to carefully excavate and record all the finds, treasure hunters take great risks in search of objects they can sell on the illegal antiquities market. Shipwreck sites can provide much more information than land sites; they are like sealed time capsules – because nothing else has been added to the site since the day the ship sank.

Important discoveries have been made on ancient shipwrecks. Here an archaeologist is examining a cargo of stone coffins, lost in the Aegean Sea over 2,000 years ago.

No, this is not the Parthenon! It is an exact life-size copy, made in the 1930s in Nashville, USA, where it is the town's museum. Ancient Greek architecture has been admired by modern architects who have used its styles in new buildings. Are there any examples in your town?

Archaeologists in Greece have to look after thousands of ancient buildings. Here you can see where new stone has been added to an old wall, preserving it for future generations.

GLOSSARY

Acropolis – A hill where Greek citizens could go for safety.

Alexander the Great (356–323 BC) – A Macedonian king and military leader who conquered the largest empire in the Ancient World. He was the son of Philip II.

Archaic Period – A short time of prosperity.

Athens – The most successful Ancient Greek city and today's capital of Greece.

Bronze Age – The time before iron was in use. Bronze was the most important metal then.

Capital – The name given to the top part of a column used in a building.

Caryatid – A female figure used as a support in a building.

Chiton – A one-piece tunic worn by women.

City-state – A self-governing Greek city and its land.

Classical Period – The time of greatest achievements for the Greeks.

Dark Ages – A time of poverty beween the Bronze Age and Archaic Period.

Delphi – A religious place where the future was foretold.

Democracy – Rule by many people (the opposite of oligarchy).

Lord Elgin (1766–1841) – British diplomat who removed sculptures from the Parthenon at Athens.

Epidavros – The site of the best-preserved Greek theatre.

Erechtheum – A small temple on the Acropolis at Athens.

Sir Arthur Evans (1851–1941) – The English archaeologist who discovered the Minoan civilization.

Golden Age – The name given to the Classical Period at Athens.

Hellenistic Period – The time of small kingdoms after the collapse of Alexander the Great's empire.

Hissarlik – The place where Schliemann found the site of ancient Troy.

Homer – A poet who lived during the Dark Ages.

Iliad – A poem by Homer about the Trojan War.

Kouroi and Kourai – The names given to early types of male and female statues.

Knossos – The site of the largest Minoan town.

Labyrinth – A maze at Knossos.

'Linear A' and **'Linear B'** – The names given to an early form of writing.

Macedonia – A region in the north of Greece.

Marathon – A land battle where a Greek army defeated a Persian army in 490 BC.

Minoan – The name given to the people who lived on Crete during the Bronze Age.

Minotaur – A creature that lived in the Labyrinth.

Mount Olympus – The mountain home of the Greek gods.

Mycenae – The site of the largest Mycenaean town.

Mycenaeans – The name given to the people who lived on mainland Greece during the Bronze Age.

Odyssey – A poem by Homer about the Trojan War.

Oligarchy – Rule by a few people (the opposite of democracy).

Olympia – The city where the Olympic Games were held.

Olympic Games – A festival of sport.

Parthenon – The largest temple on the Acropolis at Athens.

Peloponnesian War – A war between Athens and Sparta.

Pericles (about 495–429 BC) – A great Athenian statesman.

Philip II (about 382–336 BC) – A Macedonian king and military leader.

Salamis – A sea battle where a Greek navy defeated a Persian navy in 480 BC.

Heinrich Schliemann (1822–90) – The German archaeologist who discovered the Mycenaean civilization.

Shaft graves – The name given to deep graves at Mycenae.

Sparta – A rival city to Athens.

Trireme – A battleship with oars and a sail.

Trojan War – A war between Mycenaean and Trojan armies.

Troy – The capital city of the Trojans, in modern Turkey.

Michael Ventris (1922–56) – The English architect who deciphered 'Linear B' writing.

Vergina – The place where Macedonian kings were buried.

INDEX

Page numbers in **bold** refer to illustrations or their captions.

Acropolis   19, 20, **21**, 32
Akragas, temples   16
Alexander the Great   22, **22**, 23
alphabet   24, **24**
Archaic Period   16
Archimedes   26, **26**
armour   **13**, 30
army   30
Athena   32
Athens   18, 32

battle of Chaeronea   22
battle of Issus   **23**
battle of Salamis   31
Bucephalus   **22, 23**
Bronze Age   10, 11, 12

Chadwick, John   11
Charioteer of Delphi   **36**
city-states   18
clothes   29, **29**
Classical Period   20
colonies   16, 17
columns   32, **33**
creatures   39
Crete, island of   10
Cyclades, Islands   **8, 9**

Daedalus   38

Dark Ages   14
Darius III   22, **23**
Delphi   37, **37**
democracy   18, 19
doctors   **27**

Elgin, Lord   **33**
Ephesus   **42, 43**
Epidavros   **28**
Eratosthenes   26, 27
Evans, Sir Arthur   10

gods   36, 37, 43
goddesses   36, 37, 43
Golden Age   20
Gortyn   **19**, 24

Hellenistic Period   23
heroes   39
Hippocrates   27
Hissarlik   14
Homer   14, **14**
hoplites   30
hunter-gatherers   8

Icarus   38
'Iliad'   14

Knossos   10, **10**, 11

Labyrinth   39
legends   38
'Linear A' script   11
'Linear B' script   11, **11**
Lion Gate   **13**
literature   27

Macedonia   21
'Magna Graecia'   17
Marathon   30
Mask of Agamemnon   **13**
masks, theatrical   29, **29**
medicine   27
Minoan civilization   10, **10**, 11, **11**
Minotaur   39, **39**
music   28, 29
Mycenaean civilization   12, **12**, 13, **13**
myths   38

navy   31
nymphs   36

obsidian   8
'Odyssey'   14
oligarchy   21
Olympia   40, **40**
Olympic Games   40, 41
Olympus, Mount   36
Oracle of Delphi   37

Parthenon   **9, 21, 32**, **33**
Peloponnesian War   21
Pericles   20, **20**
Phaestos Disk   **11**
Philip II   21, **22, 23**
Phoenicians   24
Piraeus   20

Plato   27, **27**
poets   13
Praxiteles   **35**

religion   36, 37
Romans   40, 42

sacrifice   36
Santorini, island of   11
Schliemann, Heinrich   13, **13**
science   26
ships   31
Socrates   27
soldiers   30
Sparta   19
statues   34, 35, **35**
storytellers   13, 38

Taygetos Mountains   18, **18**
temples   32, **32**
theatre   28, **28**, 29
Thera, island of   11
Theseus   39
trireme   31, **31**
Trojan War   14, **15**
Troy   14

Ventris, Michael   11
volcano   11

wooden horse   **15**
writing   11, 24, **24**, 25

Zeus   **34, 37**

FURTHER READING

If you want to find out more about Ancient Greece, these books will help:

I Was There: Ancient Greece, John D. Clare (The Bodley Head, 1993)
Cambridge Primary History: Ancient Greece, Tim Copeland (Cambridge University Press, 1997)
Spotlights: The Ancient Greeks, Charles Freeman (Oxford University Press, 1996)
See Through History: Ancient Greece, Rowena Loverance and Tim Wood (Hamlyn, 1992)
The Greeks, Susan Peach and Anne Millard (Usborne, 1990)
Eyewitness Guides: Ancient Greece, Anne Pearson (Dorling Kindersley, 1992)